kissing caskets

KISSING CASKETS

Mahogany L. Browne

BLUE NOTE EDITION

ISBN 978-1-936919-49-9

PRINTED IN THE UNITED STATES OF AMERICA

PUBLISHED BY YESYES BOOKS
1614 NE ALBERTA ST
PORTLAND, OR 97211
YESYESBOOKS.COM

KMA SULLIVAN, PUBLISHER
JILL KOLONGOWSKI, MANAGING EDITOR
STEVIE EDWARDS, SENIOR EDITOR, BOOK DEVELOPMENT
ALBAN FISCHER, GRAPHIC DESIGNER
BEYZA OZER, DEPUTY DIRECTOR OF SOCIAL MEDIA
AMBER RAMBHAROSE, CREATIVE DIRECTOR OF SOCIAL MEDIA
PHILLIP B. WILLIAMS, COEDITOR IN CHIEF, VINYL
AMIE ZIMMERMAN, EVENTS COORDINATOR
JOANN BALINGIT, ASSISTANT EDITOR
MARY CATHERINE CURLEY, ASSISTANT EDITOR
COLE HILDEBRAND, ASSISTANT EDITOR
CARLY SCHWEPPE, ASSISTANT EDITOR, VINYL
HARI ZIYAD, ASSISTANT EDITOR, VINYL

contents

the blk(est) night

be a blk girl

she think

her hair
too good
   & her waist
    too small
     & her fit
     too cute
      & her jeans
      too flyy

& her mama ain't nothing
like her
& the bitches
on the corner
ain't nothing like her
& can't nobody sweat her style

             but Jesus

blurred vision

you & Li Li ain't talking

cause she think she   cute

cause she think   you ain't

must be pretty boy   Curtis

all in her head

all in her mouth

making her forget her home

training   making her forget

her daddy got a gun

for a living   & her mom

ain't live with them   &

this is why you think she ain't

got no sense   no how   cause

ain't nobody but fast girls

checking for Curtis

& he keep her name close
& she don't come home
            the same way no more
she must think   she cute
must think you ain't   how
she keep you waiting like
you posed to wait on Curtis—or something
& you hate his   light   skin self
            cause he ain't funny as he think
                    specially when he call you blk
                            & ugly & stupid
                                    & she stay grinning

like he the sun

like ya'll ain't friends
like you ain't protect her from them heffas that want to jump on her
every time you go to the skate rink
cause Li Li pretty   & they boyfriends forget they home training around her
so when Curtis say the thangs you already done said about yourself

9

& she laugh   you know   deep down inside   she ain't never really thought you was pretty
  no how

how she just said them lies   to keep yo shadow   up & around her sunshine   smile
  she be the sun

when you go to the pool party
& everybody there in they in bikinis
& you got your one piece with a white t-shirt on top

& the boys just'a looking
like they mama ain't taught them
nothing worth knowing

& Li Li got that good hair so she don't care if it's wet & loose
& your hair ain't close to being good

so you keep it in a tight *tight* real tight ponytail   til the sun get so hot
you jump in to cool your   sadness down
it's like you already know
so you let your shoulders sink low like your heart be

   watch Li Li   how she walk

& everybody stop

& you trynna learn

    cause ain't nobody got time for the kind of shade you got

but everybody got time for the   s u n

Li Li smile at Curtis

& he only a little bit cute

but he ain't funny or smart   so that's how you know she lying

  you pretend you don't hear his South Sacramento slur

you pretend you can't see his hazel eyes

    he say

        "lose her ugly black ass"

        & Li Li laugh   she say   "shut up, Curtis"

but it sound like   "come here"

so you dunk your head underwater   slow

&   wait   for her   to say something like:

    "don't talk about my friend, i don't care how pretty your eyes is" but she just say   "shut up"

& she laugh

& you think   *you could stay here*

where it's all a blurry aqua blue you think

                    you could stay here

where your eyes don't hurt so much

&   it don't feel like you been looking at the sun   all   day   long

shotgun suite

easy man, leave me
Forgive the cut
clean shotgun lineage
the name and mouth

stained::forgive the threat
the sliced window::oh moon,
::uncle with a mouthful of fire
and crack and blk girl demise

i beg, leave me this

of wrecking ball saunter
oh mother saint, oh holy neglect,
christen the blackness
in dark sullied sin water

once you snuck a boy into your mama's house he is the worst idea ever born this is before his box cut fade turned tornado warning smoke your trust can you see it? his crooked yellow grin/a siren alarm/your hands, crossed?

beneath you

           &   the sky of falling

green grass patch of land

                tumbling beneath your feet

the best time i had as a teenager
included a bottle of cisco and a sideshow
at the uptown gas station.

after Kenny's body was bludgeoned by his girlfriend & her two brothers

there was no one to tell us we couldn't
talk loud and follow the sound of our e c h o e s
ragged with haunt and laughter.

before Andre lived to tell about his hit & run accident at the homecoming party

when brown limbs held forty ounces and each other's ego
a delicate enchantment.

after Andre was left for dead in a stalled car a year later

the air c r a c k l e d
the tires squealed a lullaby in the emptying parking lot
we abandoned our smiles for scowls

before Shawn's body flew through the car windshield

of an unmemorable death

caked by the dust

all we knew was move drink swivel & the promise
for our kind of brown   only worthy of
                a casket
                of black bones

11

the first kiss

is a library shadowboxing midday event
is a high school sophomore fresh mouth French kiss
is a Dirty Dancing remake in the making
with a nappy headed boy named Dominque

except it is nothing like Dirty Dancing
Dominique is no Patrick Swayze

still
      you are flying
arms wide as a falling empire

you are climbing
outside of yourself
you are climbing
to the safest branch in a tree above
hands folded prim across
a white ruffled skirt
a promise of judgment braided into
your hair

no, Dominique is no Patrick Swayze

but he is here
his tongue is wet with want
you do not know he will be a father soon

and his girlfriend will call you two days from now
you will learn that his hands
always find young girls like you

but he is here now
thrusting his pelvis into yours
like a history lesson
and you thrusting back
out of context and girlhood
flipping back and back to
the safest place in your spine
your mouth a threshold of maybe
and your fingers twirling his
coily cut hair—your breath so silent
like books on the shelves
in the library
so you twirl your tongue
back and back
like the black girl perched
in the white gathers above
isn't watching

a cul de sac ain't nothing but a dead end
for the living   perfect squared houses
breed folk afraid of their own black;   us
—kin of the sharecropper writhe beneath duplex
shack shadows

like

we ain't scared of the sun

a cul de sac can bury the mouths of its young

    rinse the sorrow like hooch call it mocha

babies ain't posed to sip on dark brew

        coffee will make ya black, ya know?

grind fresh cut lemons into brown/brown flesh

wait   for baptismal burn   listen   to it sizzle

black skin on fire be a sight; watch the generations prey

a cul de sac look like a cornfield   ablaze

the darker hues   sit like jutted chin bones

holding for dark   folk tales crowd back porches

pass treaties of light   like a grandparent's hunch

—her offspring, a dollop of ash   roost & curse the sun

kerosene litany

I wish I knew how
It would feel to be free
I wish I could break
All the chains holding me
   —NINA SIMONE

today i am a black woman in america
& i am singing a melody ridden lullaby
it sound like the gentrification of a brooklyn stoop
the rent raised three times my wages
the bodega and laundromat burned down on the corner
the people on each corner
each lock and key of their chromosome
a note of inquiry on their tongue

today i am a black woman in a hopeless state
i will apply for financial aid and food stamps
with the same mouth i spit poems from
i will ask the angels of a creative god to lessen
the blows
& i will beg for forgiveness when i curse
the rising sun

today, i am a black woman in a body of coal
i am always burning and no one knows my name
i am a nameless fury, i am a blues scratched from

the throat of ms. Nina—i am always angry
i am always a bumble hive of hello
i love like this too loudly, my neighbors
think i am a unforgiving bitter
sometimes, i think my neighbors are right
most time i think my neighbors are nosy

today, i am a cold country, a storm
brewing, a heat wave of a woman wearing
red pumps to the funeral of my ex-lovers

today, i am a woman, a brown and black &
brew woman dreaming of a freedom

today, i am a mother, and my country is burning
& i forgot how to flee from such a flamboyant
backdraft
—i'm too in awe of how beautiful i look
        on fire

There are no answers   neither,
no man wrapped in the stenciling of your father no canvas large enough
to kerosene your smile   no home called home loud enough to house
your insecure   no type
of swing/sway/wander/wonder
the wind   finds you amusing

bowling alley snitch

3rd grade adoration
& Grandma wear her yellow polyester
                    something snazzy
Beautiful Chad
Every week
Light skin
        BeautifulAfroCurlyHairedChad

Pink teddy bear sweatshirt was my shit

                I told her "I like Chad face"

Grandma in her yellow polyester
Too tickled
& I don't know where the joke is

Next week
Chad say he don't want
To share my French fries
Chad don't want to be my friend
Chad don't want to sit next to me

My pinkteddybear sweatshirt go ugly
It ain't pretty no more
It's just stupid. And pink.

I look at Grandma
her gap-tooth looking back

A numb hurt so soft in my chest
I almost forget
        it live there

12 play genesis

deep amber · distant **memory** · shape is swollen · perfect brown boy · remember

your name · last crush **sings** · a lilt in his walk · his tongue wags · pale

pink & you smile · because the sun · because **darkness** · pull corners · of your

face squint · gap-tooth **hint** · smile lingers; **wager** · & you danced; · **half-moon**

—fade · your hungry hands · you, frown in the dark · his fingers · shove

between your cotton · & denim & wet **you** · frowned & he stopped · **uncertain** you, · in the dark

smell **copper** · sighed   but you, · want in · a storm · of hormones

high on endo **smoke** · everyone is **touching** · someone · no one is · frowning

& stories passed · **you** always **want** · to have **a story** · for the cold, you · don't know what it is

you **fold** each breath · like a black girl mistake · to lose **yourself** · in   a shadow · &   **wait**

16

for Miss Smith

you learn a lot about yourself when you fall into the wet mouth

of your first real boyfriend   his jheri curl moisturize your dry &

grateful hands   you are an open spout & each black girl   limb

turned a greased wing of divine god(ly) appendage   forms   praying

mantis stance   today he is making you feel   good for picking   good

for keeping   good   for more than just the wait   & for the first time since

you began this journey of spill   you cannot remember the word

ruin   instead you focus   —his fingers on your back—   how they

feel so much better than your own against   the slick pink   he must think   you

are thinking of something   less dangerous   sand brown earth

maternal advice

for Coco

I. Now

ignore your lover's name

his smile a stain smudged across everything before
him and you will only remember your grandmother
her words a flag of desperation and survival

"don't love nobody more than they love you"

II. Then

you   love   too   much
you   sing   too   much
you   laugh too   much

so loud and bright   stop

it's like you challenging the world
it's almost   like the world knows
you ain't never been worn against
nothing real

III. Soon

the clothes will wash themselves
and your hands will find the softest
folds of your body to break wet
atop the bedroom sheets each night

& then you will search for

        women poets &

    love   if they find a romance that lasts
    love   how long romance lasts when you say it s l o w
    love   if they pose on book covers a glow fire of
    "yes, i deserve this"   kind of love   &

that suggests the b o d y
is never too old to b e n d over a kitchen sink

or maybe

    they are a l o n e like you   a selfish tide
    a forgotten breath until the page holds their name
    with a lover's attention   maybe they too
                        enjoy the taste of their own
                        salty fingers in the dark

working title

The name of this poem is:

       How to write a poem about Ferguson

Or

The name of this poem is:

       How a black man dies and no one makes a sound

Or

The name of this poem is:

       Everywhere is Ferguson

Or

The name of this poem is:

       When the moonrise sounds like gunshots

Or

The name of this poem is:

       How to teach your babies to walk and not run, ever

Or

The name of this poem is:

       How to teach your babies to carry a wallet

       the size of their smile

Or

The name of this poem is:

       How to smile & not make yourself a target

Or

The name of this poem is:

       How to write a poem the same size of Emmett Till's lungs

Or

The name of this poem is:

       How to write a poem about America's thirst

Or

The name of this poem is:

       Black blood'll keep you thirsty

Or

The name of this poem is:

       I'm still thirsty, An American Horror Story

Or

The name of this poem is:

       How to write an escape route from a tornado

Or

The name of this poem is:

       How to write an escape route
       when the tornado's name is Stop & Frisk

Or

The name of this poem is:

       How walk the streets without fearing
       someone will cut your neck open

Or

       How to walk into a boardroom
       without fearing someone will cut your legacy open

Or

       How to walk without asking for it

Or

       How to walk without asking for it

Or

       How to determine what "asking for it" looks like

Or

The name of this poem is:

How "asking for it" feel like a church bombing

Or

The name of this poem is:

How to not intimidate nobody in 3 small steps

Or

The name of this poem is:

How to use your science books as Teflon

& how that still might not work

Or

The name of this poem is:

How to write about the one time you held a gun

Or

The name of this poem is:

How write about the one time you had a gun pointed to your face

Or

The name of this poem is:

How write about the one time you had a gun pointed to your face

Or

The name of this poem is:

How write about the one time you had a gun pointed to your face

Or

The name of this poem is:

How write about the one time you had a gun pointed to your face

Or

The name of this poem is:

How to write a poem from the perspective of a cop's gun

a cop's Taser

a cop's baton

a cop's boot

Or

The name of this poem is:

How to write poem without r e p e a t i n g yourself

moon mouth

my mouth became the moon/ found a way to fly up/up & a ways/   like
a star. no, like a moon. & some/one said i should shine like that/all glow.
no. my body should be silent like a bullet./or./no. like a star./a dead spark
—if you look close enough   & then/just like that—my mouth   eclipsed

a tacit & clean suture./. . . where my face be

the second

you come from a place where boys hunt new *tittified* frames
& Clifton was always hunting something/ them eyes bugged out
seeing everything that ain't want to be noticed

he scavenge your new permed hair
scour across your redred lipstick
& wait

> you tell him *i ain't fast*
> you tell him *i ain't trynna kiss all up on you*
> you reapply the redred lip smudge
> &   think *i might as well since he lookin'*

besides, you already done snuck the stain
from your big sister's purse/redred lip always
had a way of making black girls feel like Marilyn Monroe

& you wasn't trynna really BE Clifton's girlfriend no how
'cept he ain't hearing you/ he only lookin'
& now ya'll in front of your mama's house
on top of her once white 4-door cutlass hooptie

& Clifton pry open your legs   he say *give me a hug*

& your cousin Niecey say *do it*
& your lips say *be like Marilyn*

            like that one movie where she pout & shimmy & sing
            'bout diamonds   & you ain't never seen diamonds
            but you practice the shimmy & pout when nobody lookin'

he wait

            then you break
            each arm a welcome float
you still   he wait
& you hug him like you want to be hugged
you say   promise you leave *me alone now*
he murmur something that sound like   *maybe*
before his long mouth scoot in your direction
& you think   *well, we here ain't we*
& you try to dip your head like the pretty girls in the movies
except he don't hug like a warm bath   he wrap around
your body tight   a bear trap

dear daughter

a black woman with eyes like ours
is always prey

notes

12 Play genesis was informed by the poem "When 12 Play was on Repeat." The genesis form was created by Cave Canem alum and retreat faculty Amanda Johnston.

- There are five individual poems in each column (Left to Right)
- The 6th poem is the entire body of the poem (Left to Right or Right to Left)
- The 7th poem is an erasure poem compiled of the bold words (Left to Right)

acknowledgments

For Amari, always in your name, I write.

Forever my love to Serenbe Air & Sarah Kay, Cave Canem & Nicole Sealey, Poets House & Ocean Vuong, for fellowship and community space to gather my thoughts. To Jive Poetic, Falu, Whitney Greenaway, Eve Ewing, Jason Reynolds, Kevin Young, Kevin Coval, Adam Falkner, Cristin O'Keefe Aptowicz, Manny Montana, Charlotte Sheedy, Krista Franklin, Christian Hawkeye, Anna Moschovakis, KMA Sullivan, Idrissa Simmonds, Yesenia Montilla, Rachel Eliza Griffiths, Sonia Sanchez, Tongo Eisen Martin, Eboni Hogan, Ursula Rucker & the fighters, teachers & poets that keep me writing when the world is too tough. To the elders that came before me and the young that will rise with these poems.

Thank you

Kerosene Litany originally published by Academy of American Poets
Working Title originally published in *Winter Tangerine*
the blk(est) night and **blurred vision** originally published in *SMUDGE* (Button Poetry)

A Cave Canem, Poets House & Serenbe Focus alum, **Mahogany L. Browne** is the author of several books including *Redbone* (nominated for NAACP Outstanding Literary Works), and *Dear Twitter: Love Letters Hashed Out Online* (recommended by Small Press Distribution and About. com Best Poetry Books of 2010). Browne has toured Germany, Amsterdam, England, Canada and recently Australia as 1/3 of the cultural arts exchange project Global Poetics. Her poetry has been published in literary journals *Pluck, Manhattanville Review, Muzzle, Union Station Mag, Literary Bohemian, Bestiary,* and *The Feminist Wire.* She is the author of an illustrated book *Black Girl Magic* (Roaring Brook Press 2018), co-editor of forthcoming anthology *The Break Beat Poets: Black Girl Magic,* and the Artistic Director of Urban Word NYC (as seen on HBO's *Brave New Voices*). She is founder of Women Writers of Color Reading Room & working with Black Lives Matter Program at Pratt Institute. Browne is also the publisher of Penmanship Books, the Nuyorican Poets Café Friday Night Slam curator, and recent graduate from Pratt Institute MFA Writing & Activism program.

Also from YesYes Books